GREAT BUILDINGS OF
SAN FRANCISCO
A Photographic Guide

ROBERT C. BERNHARDI

Dover Publications, Inc.
New York

Published in Canada by General Publishing Company, Ltd., 30 Lesmill Road, Don Mills, Toronto, Ontario.
Published in the United Kingdom by Constable and Company, Ltd., 10 Orange Street, London WC2H 7EG.

Great Buildings of San Francisco: A Photographic Guide is a new work, first published by Dover Publications, Inc., in 1980.

International Standard Book Number: 0-486-23839-3
Library of Congress Catalog Card Number: 79-51660

Manufactured in the United States of America
Dover Publications, Inc.
180 Varick Street
New York, N.Y. 10014

INTRODUCTION

Accounts of a visitor in the early 1800s describe San Francisco as a barren collection of huts, a condition that was true of all other communities of California at that time except Monterey, the capital city.

Perhaps overlooked by the visitor was Mission Dolores, an adobe church completed in 1791 near a streambed in the present heart of the city. Rundown at the time, Mission Dolores was to be the only architecturally significant building in San Francisco until the middle of the nineteenth century.

From the 1850s, the city was engulfed in a wave of Classical Revival structures replacing the wooden shacks that burned with frequency. (Forty-niners, in a hurry to set up shop, even went so far as to operate businesses out of ships beached in the Bay; the *Niantic*, whose hull was recently excavated under a downtown building site, is one example.)

In nondomestic architecture, Classical Revival, replete with pillars, pediments and pedestals, lasted well into the twentieth century. Then terra-cotta-clad structures of high elevation, representing modified Gothic, Art Deco, Mediterranean and other styles, became the dominant mode. Architecture of the 1930s gave way, with few exceptions, to the impersonal rectangles and monoliths that now dominate the skylines of most large American cities.

The forty-six nondomestic structures that make up this book might be considered prototypes of these styles. The selection of "great buildings" is, of course, somewhat subjective (and any such list is bound to be subject to disagreement). The criteria used for their inclusion, however, were not. Not only were the buildings chosen because of inherent visual interest, but each of them has been noted in previous architectural surveys of San Francisco, such as the study undertaken by the Junior League and Historical Sites Project in the 1960s. Although a few are deteriorating, most are in good-to-excellent condition, some having undergone recent restoration. Fortunately, none has been altered for a more "modern" appearance.

It is also fortunate that none of the structures, at this writing at least, is in danger of demolition. Historic preservation is not a dirty term in San Francisco, thanks to the untiring efforts of the Landmarks Preservation Advisory Board, The Foundation for San Francisco's Architectural Heritage, and other organizations. Needless to say, vigilance is still necessary. Most of the forty-six buildings included here were dominant on the skyline for decades; many are now lost in a forest of high rises and need to be ferreted out. Unless otherwise credited, I have taken the photographs presented here. To facilitate location, I have arranged the buildings by geographical area. They can be located by number on the accompanying map.

I would like to thank Keith Dills for reading the manuscript and suggesting alterations; Carol Olwell for her advice on miscellaneous book matters; the staff of the Special Collections Department of the San Francisco Public Library; the Art Department of the Oakland Public Library; and the Bancroft and Environmental Design Libraries of the University of California at Berkeley.

Oakland, 1979   Robert C. Bernhardi

MAP OF SAN FRANCISCO

The boldface numbers show the approximate locations
of the forty-six buildings discussed.

Basic map reproduced by permission of the California State Automobile Association, copyright owner.

CONTENTS

GREAT BUILDINGS OF
SAN FRANCISCO
A Photographic Guide

PRESIDIO/MARINA/RICHMOND

These three areas at the northwestern edge of San Francisco, originally the most barren in the city, were covered with sand dunes when the first settlers arrived. The Presidio, oldest of the three, dates to 1776, the year of the first encampment of Spanish-Mexican forces. The Marina, fronting along the Bay, was developed on land used for the 1915 Panama-Pacific Exposition. Relatively flat Richmond, south of the Presidio, filled up with row houses between 1910 and 1930, on the windy and foggy dunes. Today, the Marina and Richmond districts contain some of the city's most desirable residences.

FORT POINT

Fort Point, prominently located at the entrance to San Francisco Bay, has the distinction of being the northernmost building in the city.

Castillo de San Joaquín was constructed by the Spaniards at this location in 1794. Built in the form of a horseshoe, the fort had ten-foot-thick adobe walls. Bronze cannons, cast in the seventeenth century in Lima, Peru, reminded mariners that they could enter the Bay only by the grace of King Carlos III of Spain. One of the original twelve cannons can still be seen at the fort.

By the time the subsequent Mexican occupation of Yerba Buena (San Francisco) had ended in 1846, Castillo de San Joaquín was in a state of ruin. In 1853, the old fort was torn down, the site leveled, and construction of a new American fort begun. It was completed in 1861 at a cost of $2.8 million. Constructed along the lines of Fort Sumter, Fort Point is considered one of the best examples of fortification architecture of the 1850s.

Granite quarried from Folsom, California, and from as far away as China, was used for the base. The upper stories were constructed of bricks made by prisoners at San Quentin. Other bricks were made at a factory on Russian Hill.

The irregularly shaped interior courtyard is surrounded on three of its four sides with galleries of tiered arches. The granite stairways are quite elegant; each stair is supported solely by the weight of the immediately underlying block of granite.

The galleries originally held offices, living quarters and a hospital. The first floor had a small stockade and quartermaster's quarters. Cast-iron railings surround the gallery walkways. Embedded in the wood doors are large cast-iron studs to discourage forced entry.

In 1882, the fort was renamed Fort Winfield Scott. By 1905, it was considered obsolete, and a new fort was started nearby. In 1914, old Fort Point was abandoned. It came to life again in World War I, when it was used to house German prisoners. During World War II, a searchlight and gun battery were added to the fort's defenses (which, incidentally, have never been used). After the war, Fort Point became rundown again. The House Interior and Insular Affairs Committee authorized $52 million to restore the fort in 1970; restoration efforts were completed the following year. Now a National Historic Site, the fort is under the administration of the National Park Service.

Opposite: Fort Point. **Left:** A seventeenth-century Peruvian cannon in the courtyard. Above is the Golden Gate Bridge. (*Photograph by Richard Frear, courtesy the U.S. Department of the Interior*). **Below:** A door studded to resist forced entry. **Bottom, left:** A detail of the granite spiral staircase. **Bottom, right:** Arched vaults in the galleries.

2
PALACE OF FINE ARTS

Looming over the Marina District, like some ancient Roman ruin, stands the Palace of Fine Arts, Baker Street and Marina Boulevard, built for the city's Panama-Pacific Exposition of 1915. It has become for San Francisco what the Eiffel Tower became for Paris following its 1889 exhibition and what the Crystal Palace became for London after its Great Exhibition of 1851—a structure that lived on long after the original fair to become an integral part of the city.

In part a celebration of the quick reconstruction of San Francisco after the devastating earthquake of 1906, the Panama-Pacific Exposition had as its main purposes the commemoration of the four-hundredth anniversary of the discovery of the Pacific Ocean by the explorer Balboa and the completion of the Panama Canal in 1914. The uniformly Classical architectural style of the exposition was a throwback to the World's Columbian Exposition, held in Chicago in 1893.

The architect chosen for the Palace of Fine Arts, Bernard R. Maybeck, had achieved fame in 1910 for his First Christian Science Church of Berkeley. Maybeck's design called for the Palace complex—a rotunda, peristyle and art gallery—to be constructed on the edge of a lagoon, so that the structure would be reflected in the water as well as silhouetted against the sky. The focal point is the massive octagonal rotunda standing in the midpoint of a semicircular free-standing peristyle that borders the lagoon. Behind these colonnades is the Palace itself, a 1100-foot-long, arc-shaped art gallery. Allan Temko, the architecture critic, sums up Maybeck's work here best: "... yet the brooding dome and monumental splendor of the Palace of Fine Arts ... reveal what Maybeck really dreamed of as great architecture. The grandeur of the past, as he learned it, at the Ecole des Beaux-Arts in Paris, but suffused with his personal romanticism."[1]

The columns of the rotunda and peristyle are Corinthian. Large Roman-style urns surround the rotunda's base. Statues atop the peristyle, one at each corner of structures that were originally intended (but never used) as planters, are of seemingly weeping figures, which help convey the mood Maybeck strove for: "... an old Roman ruin, away from civilization which two thousand years before was the center of action and full of life, and is now partly overgrown with bushes and trees—such ruins give the mind a sense of sadness."[2] Indeed, the "bushes and trees" were integral to the Palace; such landscape helped to tie the structures together. The entire grouping was meant to produce an effect of great tranquility tinged with sadness, which it does to this day.

Unfortunately, the structures were not intended to be permanent. The rotunda and peristyles were made of wood covered with burlap and fiber. The Palace, which had a skylight that illuminated 120 exhibition rooms, was walled with cement. Maybeck stated, "If left alone the Palace of Fine Arts will outlast us. It has cost $700,000."[3] But he was wrong. The structure, the only one left standing after the exposition, did, in fact, begin to crumble. San Franciscans, however, were far too fond of it to tear it down and the Palace was put to various uses: in the 1930s, eighteen lighted tennis courts were installed on the grounds; it was used as a motor pool during World War II; in the early 1950s it housed the city's art festival.

Finally, in 1957, $2 million was given by the state for demolition and reconstruction. In 1959, philanthropist Walter S. Johnson offered another $2 million. The same year the citizens voted a bond issue of $1 million. In 1964, the original structures began to be dismantled and models made to aid with reconstruction. Work continued off and on until 1975, when the complex was completed. The gallery area now contains the Exploratorium and the Palace of Fine Arts Theatre.

[1]Temko, Allan. "The West's First Modern Architecture," *San Francisco Chronicle*, January 30, 1978, p. 6.
[2]Maybeck, Bernard R. *Palace of Fine Arts and Lagoon*. San Francisco: Paul Elder and Co., 1915, p. 10.
[3]*Architect and Engineer*, November 1915, p. 15.

Top: The Palace of Fine Arts and the Lagoon. **Above, left:**
The peristyle is topped by planter boxes and statues of weeping women. **Above, right:** The people give an idea of the
rotunda's massive size.

3

TEMPLE EMANU-EL

Temple Emanu-El, at Arguello and Lake Boulevards, is the third building to house this historic congregation. The first structure was built in 1850 on old Broadway, shortly after Jewish forty-niners founded the congregation. An impressive Sutter Street edifice was completed in the mid-1860s, but was seriously damaged in the 1906 conflagration. In 1926 the Reformed Congregation left that home and dedicated its current house of worship.

Architects for the new cream-colored stucco temple were Sylvain Schnaittacher, John Bakewell and Arthur Brown; Bernard Maybeck and Albert Landsburgh, consultants. The Byzantine style was chosen for its Near Eastern flavor, and for its use of the dome, a prominent feature of many Jewish structures. The temple also has a definite California Mission flavor as expressed in its arches, tiles and courtyard.

The temple is entered through a gateway which opens onto a Byzantine-Roman court. Arches at the side are supported by fluted columns with lion's-head capitals. Above each capital is a fish-scale design. In the center of the court is a fountain whose basin is ornamented with lion's-head waterspouts. Above the central porch are two larger lions' heads supporting columns and an arch which forms a niche for the everlasting light. Above the arch are the two Tables of the Law, on which are inscribed the first words of the Ten Commandments in Hebrew.

A striking feature of the interior is the vestibule. The vaulted ceiling is painted cerulean blue, with an octagonal design traced in yellow-gold. At each end are two columns of verde antique marble. Four lamps, with bases of travertine marble, stand next to the wall.

The upper part of the 1700-seat auditorium is surrounded on three sides by latticework balconies which are in turn supported by Byzantine columns of verde antique marble. Light enters the auditorium through two large windows of antique glass.

Supported by four great arches, the dome rises one hundred fifty feet from the ground. Its russet-tile exterior contrasts nicely with the California sky. It is possible to climb the interior of the drum of the dome, from which a splendid view of the city can be enjoyed.

Opposite, left: The central porch. **Opposite, right:** The west cloister. **Above:** Temple Emanu-El. **Right:** The congregation's previous synagogue, seen in a view ca. 1870, stood on the north side of Sutter Street, between Powell and Stockton Streets. (*Courtesy The Bancroft Library*).

4
ROOSEVELT
JUNIOR HIGH SCHOOL

Roosevelt Junior High School, 460 Arguello Boulevard, was constructed in 1935 and is architects Miller and Pflueger's only brick building in San Francisco. It is a gem of fine brickwork, inspired by German and Dutch Expressionist architecture of the 1910s and 1920s. At this writing, Roosevelt Junior High is undergoing restoration with funds provided by the Field Act Reconstructions Program.

Opposite: Roosevelt Junior High School.
Above, left: Detail, south tower. **Above, right:**
Detail, central tower. **Left:** A detail of the
front wall shows copper spandrels above the
windows.

SAN FRANCISCO GAS LIGHT COMPANY BUILDING

The former San Francisco Gas Light Company Building, Buchanan and North Point Streets, is San Francisco's finest surviving brick structure in the Queen Anne/Richardson–Romanesque style. The Gas Light Company was established in 1873 by the merger of various smaller companies with the San Francisco Gas Company, which had been founded in 1852 by forty-niner Peter Donahue and his brother James. Peter later became president of the company; in 1885 the presidency passed to Joseph Crockett, who designed the present structure, which was completed in 1893. The first floor housed the company headquarters; to the rear was a large room which held two compression cylinders. On the second floor were the living quarters of the plant manager.

In 1905, the company was absorbed by the Pacific Gas and Electric Company, which held it until 1958, when the building was acquired by Merryvale, Inc., antique dealers. William Wurster of Wurster, Bernardi and Emmons did the restoration. The main room to the rear is the most striking: 28 feet high, with tall, arched windows of rolled glass. The walls are of exposed brick and contrast with the coffered beamed ceiling. The especially fine brickwork of the facade is punctuated by semicircular arched windows on the first story, a semicircular arch framing the recessed doorway, and flattened arched windows on the second story.

NOB HILL

The invention of the cable car by Andrew Hallidie in 1873 overcame the problems of riding up San Francisco's steep hills, and opened up the area adjacent to downtown to the "nabobs," from whom Nob Hill derives its name. These men were the Crockers, Hopkinses, Huntingtons, Floods, Fairs and other millionaires who built their "palaces on the hills." The earthquake of 1906 leveled all the mansions with the exception of Flood's, now the Pacific Union Club. Today, elegance and wealth exude from Nob Hill, site of some of the nation's foremost hotels.

6
GHIRARDELLI SQUARE

Ghirardelli Square, a remarkably uniform group of red brick-faced buildings surrounding an irregular courtyard, has become one of the city's major tourist and shopping attractions.

Covering a full city block bounded by North Point, Polk, Larkin and Beach Streets, the Square gets its name from Domingo Ghirardelli, an early San Francisco chocolate manufacturer whose factory occupied the major structures fronting North Point Street: the Cocoa (1900), Chocolate (1911), Mustard (1911) and Clock Tower (1915) buildings. The most interesting structure is the last named, designed by architect William Mooser, Jr. The tower itself is based on the one designed by Mansart for the Château of Blois in the seventeenth century. Rising four stories, it is distinguished by ornate cornices at the tower's base and roofline, elegantly framed mullioned windows, and by a steep mansard roof with a double finial and louvered dormers.

Three other buildings on the red-brick "square" are the Pioneer Woolen Mill Building (1860) designed by William Mooser, Sr., the old Power House (1915) and the Apartment Building (1916).

Contemporary buildings completing the courtyard were designed by the architectural firm of Wurster, Bernardi and Emmons to complement the older structures. The inviting courtyard itself has a handsome circular fountain of mermaids, frogs and tortoises sculptured by the local artist Ruth Asawa.

In 1966, Ghirardelli Square received a special award from the American Institute of Architects.

Opposite: Ghirardelli Square revitalized the base of Russian Hill. (*Courtesy Ghirardelli Square*). **Above, left:** Entrance to the tower building. **Above, right:** Ruth Asawa's Mermaid Fountain (*Courtesy Ghirardelli Square*). **Right:** The Château of Blois provided the inspiration for the clock tower.

GRACE CATHEDRAL

Grace Cathedral's origins go back to 1849, when San Francisco's first Episcopal congregation was formed. In 1863, the Rt. Reverend William Kip, the first Episcopal bishop in California, established his chair in a new masonry structure on California and Stockton Streets, which then became the first Episcopal cathedral seat in the country. The building was destroyed in the fire of 1906. Charles Crocker's elaborate mansion a few blocks away at Taylor Street on Nob Hill was also destroyed. His heirs deeded the land to the Church and, in 1914, the Founders' Crypt of the new structure was opened.

The architect was Lewis Hobart, who decided to construct the cathedral of steel and poured concrete as protection against earthquakes. Having traveled throughout Europe, his inspiration was drawn mainly from the Gothic cathedrals of Chartres, Amiens and Notre Dame (notably the twin towers and flèche or spire). Significant differences such as the omission of flying buttresses and reduction of ornamentation are attributable to the use of concrete.

Like the great cathedrals of Europe, work on Grace proceeded slowly. World War I stopped construction and work resumed in 1928 with the Chapel of Grace, on the corner of California and Jones Streets. However, the Depression brought a halt to construction in 1933, when only 60 percent of the main section of the cathedral had been completed. The unfinished nave was closed off from 1933 until 1961, when construction again resumed. The enlarged nave and second tower were added when the cathedral was completed in 1964. Architects were Weihe, Frick and Kruse.

The cathedral is 119 feet wide from buttress to buttress and 320 feet long. The twin towers rise 170 feet from the ground. At 92 feet, the nave is reputedly higher than any English cathedral's except York and Liverpool. The copper flèche is topped with a gilt cross that had to be raised into position by a huge crane. Its top is 265 feet above the cathedral's ground level.

The 44 bells of the north tower, given by Dr. Nathaniel Coulson in 1938, were cast in Croydon, England. They hung for a year at the Golden Gate Exposition on Treasure Island in 1939, after which they were transferred to the then-detached north tower.

The interior is replete with marble and stained-glass windows. The twentieth-century rose window was designed by Gabriel Loire in Chartres, using one-inch-thick faceted glass. Traditional leaded-glass windows were designed by Charles Connock of Philadelphia, who used the blue glass of Chartres as his inspiration. A third set of windows was executed by Willet of Philadelphia.

Of special interest are the Ghiberti Doors at the entrance, cast from molds taken from Lorenzo Ghiberti's "Doors of Paradise" on the Baptistery of Florence. The scenes are taken from the Old Testament, with side panels of Old Testament characters and portraits of Ghiberti and his contemporaries.

Opposite: The Ghiberti Doors, cast from molds of the originals at the Baptistery in Florence.
Above: Grace Cathedral, showing both towers and flèche.

8

FAIRMONT HOTEL

World-famous, Nob Hill was named after the "nabobs" who built their palaces there in the 1870s—railroad kings such as Stanford, Huntington, Hopkins and Crocker and the U.S. Senator James G. Fair. Fair was called a bonanza king for the fortune he had made from the Comstock Mines. (Other bonanza kings included James C. Flood, John McKay and W. S. O'Brian.)

After Fair's death in 1894, his son-in-law, Herman Oelrichs, devised plans for the construction of a major hotel. His wife, Tessie Fair, built the hotel on family property on Mason and California Streets, directly opposite the Pacific Union Club. Construction of the lavish hostelry, named in honor of Fair, began in 1903. The architects selected for the job were James and Merritt Reid, who designed the hotel in the Italian Renaissance style, which was then enjoying a vogue in the design of large buildings. Shortly thereafter Mrs. Oelrichs sold the hotel to the Law

Brothers, who had made their fortune in patent medicine.

The hotel was scheduled to open in early May of 1906. Crates of expensive furniture had been moved into the lobby. When the quake and fire hit, the entire building was gutted; only the walls survived. Restoration of the interior was supervised by the famous New York architectural firm of McKim, Mead and White and the hotel was ready for opening in April 1907. The six hundred rooms were outfitted with expensive mahogany furniture; each had its own design of heavy French wallpaper and its own bath.

Today, the hotel looks much as it did when it opened with the exception of a tower that was built to the east of the structure in 1961 to provide additional rooms and a bar with a spectacular view of the city.

Below: The Fairmont Hotel. **Opposite, top:** The lobby, as restored by McKim, Mead and White. (*Courtesy Fairmont Hotel*). **Opposite, bottom:** The gutted Fairmont can be seen at the upper-right corner of this photograph, taken after the disaster of 1906. The ruins of St. Mary's and Grace Cathedral are also visible. (*Courtesy The Bancroft Library*).

The Fairmont is constructed of white granite. A porte cochère (covered porch) stands at the Mason Street entrance, flanked on each side by Ionic columns. The main floor has tall arched windows; square windows line the second floor. From the third to sixth floors, the windows are pedimented and "supported" by columns. Six Corinthian columns line the center facade from the third floor to the sixth.

The opulent lobby is furnished in marble and velvet and decorated in tones of gold and red. The lobby space is broken up by handsome marble Corinthian columns. Ceilings are vaulted. The sumptuous room is enhanced by Florentine mirrors mounted in carved frames, inlaid with gold leaf, that were imported from Italy.

PACIFIC UNION CLUB

The Nob Hill structure at 1000 California Street was designed by Augustus Laver for James Flood, a New Yorker who arrived in San Francisco in 1849. After opening a saloon on Market Street, Flood became wealthy when he acquired silver mines in the Comstock. In 1873, the mines brought in a bonanza, and Flood opened his own Nevada Bank in 1875. After a trip East, where he saw the elegant brownstone mansions of New York City, Flood decided that his "palace" would be made out of that material. The original site on Nob Hill was an unlevel lot covered with sand and shrubbery. At great expense, the brownstone was transported piece by piece from a Connecticut quarry, shipped as ballast on a boat sent around the Horn. The 42-room mansion was completed in 1886, after two years of construction at a cost of $1.5 million. The architecture is Italian Baroque in style. Originally the home was asymmetrically balanced around a tower in the then popular "Italian villa" style.

The mansion had been so solidly built that it was the only one on Nob Hill to remain standing after the earthquake. Immediately after the disaster, ownership passed to the Pacific Union Club, an amalgam of two early San Francisco "gentlemen's clubs," the Pacific Club and the Union Club. A half-million-dollar renovation was done by Willis Polk in which the tower was removed, a third story was added to the house's original two, as well as semicircular one-story wings. Polk's skillful renovations are virtually unnoticeable from the exterior, since the additional stone used for the restoration was mined from the same quarry in Connecticut that had been used when the mansion was first built.

Since then there have been few changes. The house is surrounded by a fence of brownstone pillars and graceful metal tracery that reputedly cost $30,000. The first-story windows are rounded at the top and pedimented. Pilasters are on each side of the windows. Balustrades appear above the roofline and over the porch. Quoins (corner stones) ornament each of the four corners of the main building. The hall on the first floor (the original focus of the Flood home) and stairwell are illuminated during the day by a skylight. The hall and vestibule are lined with marble. Ionic columns, a frescoed ceiling and a grand staircase remain as in the original design.

10

THE CANNERY

The Cannery is located at 2801 Leavenworth Street, just a few blocks away from Ghirardelli Square. It is another successful adaptation of old brick buildings to modern use as a shopping center.

The Cannery was originally a three-story building used by the Del Monte Fruit Company. The architects, Esherick, Homsey, Dodge and Davis, left the exterior walls of the pre-1906 structure intact, but subdivided the main building into separate but connecting buildings. The interiors, however, are completely new.

The architects intended the Cannery to be reminis-

cent of a European open-air marketplace, and have succeeded admirably. Inside, the maze of shops and restaurants is connected by walks, corridors and escalators. An outside elevator takes patrons to the arcades on the upper levels. The landscaping, which adds a soft contrast to the more somber brick, was done by Thomas Church.

The commercial success of both the Cannery and Ghirardelli Square proves that shopping centers need not necessarily be endlessly sprawling affairs in the suburbs.

COGSWELL COLLEGE

Above: Cogswell College's Swig Hall was originally built for the Metropolitan Life Insurance Company. **Below:** The illuminated facade at night.

Cogswell College occupies the terra-cotta-clad building on the block bordered by Stockton, Pine and California Streets. It was built in 1909 for the Metropolitan Life Insurance Company as their Western headquarters, and occupies the site of the first Grace Cathedral. The building was sold to Cogswell College in 1974.

The Stockton Street wing of the building was designed by Pierre and Michel LeBrun. The impressive facade is pure Classical Revival: massive Doric columns support a pediment adorned with Classical figures; a patterned frieze completely encircles the building. The main two-story hall inside the entrance has a handsome colonnade that supports a gilt ceiling. The Pine Street wing was added in 1930; the California Street wing in 1954.

FINANCIAL DISTRICT

Much of San Francisco's financial district is built on land reclaimed from the Bay, where, over 125 years ago, boats were abandoned as frenzied travelers rushed to the goldfields in the Mother Lode. Most of the city's high rises are located here. Up until the early 1960s, San Francisco's skyline was unique, with only a few buildings, including the Russ and Shell, poking up into the sky. Subsequent construction, however, has "Manhattanized" the city's profile into a proliferation of towering skyscrapers.

TRANSAMERICA BUILDING
(Old Fugazi Bank)

The glistening Transamerica Building (not be confused with the newer Transamerica Tower) is wedged into a corner lot at Columbus and Montgomery Streets. It was built in 1911 for the Banca Popolare Italiana Operaia Fugazi, known more simply as the Old Fugazi Bank.

The Old Fugazi Bank eventually came under the control of a rival Italian bank, A. P. Giannini's Bank of Italy, which later became the largest financial institution in the country—the Bank of America. In the 1930s, the Old Fugazi Bank closed, but was used occasionally to train new employees for the Bank of America. Finally, in 1938, it became headquarters for the Transamerica Corporation, another Giannini entreprise.

The building was a two-story structure when it was erected, although architect Charles Paff had intended it to be five stories. In 1914, however, the original cupola was removed and a third story was added.

The building construction is steel frame, stone and concrete. The terra-cotta exterior is basically Classical Revival. On the first floor, tall arched windows are separated by fluted Ionic pilasters which rise to the top of the second-story windows. Scrolled

Opposite: The Transamerica Building, formerly the Fugazi Bank. **Above:** A detail of the terra-cotta facade.

keystones crown the arches. Wide, almost square windows with projecting sills are decorated with cast-iron railings.

A large dentilled cornice at the third-story level is interspaced with animal heads. Above is the rather plain third-floor facade, topped with a balustrade.

Since the demolition of the Crocker Building in 1967, along with Columbus Tower and the Phelan Building, the Transamerica Building is one of the very few "flatiron" structures remaining in San Francisco.

13

THE PACIFIC GAS
AND ELECTRIC COMPANY

The Pacific Gas and Electric Company's origins can be traced back to 1852, when Peter Donahue founded the San Francisco Gas Company, and to 1879, when the California Electric Company was formed. Until 1971, the company's main office was at this granite building, 245 Market Street. The architects, Bakewell and Brown, arranged the composition to contrast harmoniously with its adjoining neighbor, the Matson Building. The seventeen-story structure was erected on wooden piles sunk into the mud of what was originally Yerba Buena Cove. It opened in March 1925.

The building is divided into three separate elements: a base, shaft and columns topped by two recessed stories. The base runs up through the first three stories. The tall arched entrance on Market Street is decorated with Edgar Walter's sculptures symbolizing the electric power industry. Sculptured keystones surmount the arches on the high windows, extending through the second story, on both the Market and Beale Street facades. The unornamented facade of the next ten stories above the base becomes a main shaft or pedestal for the columns and arcade of the fourteenth and fifteenth floors.

In 1971, the new steel-and-granite 34-story headquarters tower was erected behind the Market Street building, adding more than one million square feet of office space to the older building. The 492-foot tower was designed by the San Francisco architectural firm of Hertzka and Knowles. Its main entrance, at 77 Beale Street, between Market and Mission Streets, is set back 35 feet from both streets' curbs, allowing for landscaping and a working waterfall.

Left: Detail of the entrance with sculpture by Edgar Walter.
Opposite: The Pacific Gas and Electric Company Building.

14
THE HYATT REGENCY HOTEL

San Francisco is fortunate in having two great hotel interiors with skylights: the Hyatt Regency, at 5 Embarcadero, just off Market Street, and the Garden Court of the Palace. The spectacular Hyatt Regency is the work of John Portman, the Atlanta-based architect-developer who has built hotels in other major U.S. cities and invested $40 million in this venture.

The triangular lobby's dimensions give a clue to its overpowering presence: over 300 feet in length, 170 feet in width, rising to a breathtaking 170 feet in height. Surrounding the atrium-court are 100 trees and 15,000 ivy plants hanging from balconies. The galleries, leading to guest rooms, are reached by five futuristic glass-enclosed cylindrical elevators, which ascend to the rooftop restaurant.

The focal point of the enormous room is an aluminum-tubed geometric sculpture by Charles O. Perry, soaring 40 feet above a black reflective pool. Nearby are plush leather chairs and couches sunken in conversation pits. Surrounding the lobby are various shops.

Less spectacular than the lobby, but still striking, is the Hyatt Regency's exterior. Seen from the north, the facade slopes inward 45° in a stepped arrangement of tiers.

Above: The north facade. **Opposite:** The atrium-lobby. (*Courtesy the Hyatt Regency Hotel*).

GARDEN COURT OF THE PALACE HOTEL

The Garden Court of the Palace hotel, 633 Market Street, is unquestionably one of the most magnificent dining rooms in the world. The massive room, which can seat 950, rises 48 feet from its marble floors to its arched glass skylight, and measures 85 by 100 feet. Sunlight filtering through the skylight's iridescent glass casts an amber glow over the room by day. At night illumination is provided by ten large and ten smaller crystal chandeliers, reportedly valued at up to $50,000 each. The walls of the room, punctuated by elaborate doorways, are resplendent with ivory-toned woodwork, gilt mirrors and sconces and Italian-marble Ionic pillars.

The original Palace Hotel, completed in 1875, was financed by two entrepreneurs, William Sharon and William Ralston. Ralston, an ex-riverboat captain from the East, came West to found the Bank of California. Sharon was a U.S. Senator from Nevada. The men pooled resources, and, for five million dollars, built the largest hotel in the West: 750 rooms, each with fireplace and water closet. Shortly before the hostelry's opening, however, the Bank of California collapsed, and Ralston drowned himself.

The seven-story edifice was decorated with 50,000 yards of French carpeting and furniture of mahogany, rosewood, teak and ebony. But the hotel's unique feature was the Grand or Carriage Court, a circular driveway surrounded by tiered balconies, rising seven stories to a glass roof supported by trusses. Visitors alighted from their coaches into the palm-studded court. Some hired carriages just to make "the grand entrance."

Famous guests who sojourned in the hotel included: King David Kalakaua, the last of the Hawaiian kings, who died there; Emperor Dom Pedro II of Brazil, who came in 1876; General Sherman; Oscar Wilde; Sarah Bernhardt; Anna Held; Lillian Russell and Ignace Paderewski. Enrico Caruso allegedly fell out of his bed there during the quake.

While the 1906 earthquake did little damage to the structure, the ensuing fire gutted it. A new hotel was built on the same location in 1909; the designers were Trowbridge and Livingston, imported from

Left: The Carriage Court of the old Palace Hotel in the 1880s. (*Courtesy The Bancroft Library*). **Opposite:** The present interior of the Garden Court.

New York City. This time the court was made into a grand dining room, rising to the third story. In the years since its construction, it has also been used for symphony concerts, theatrical events and other functions.

In the "new" hotel, President Woodrow Wilson made a speech in 1919 urging American support of the League of Nations. President Harding died here in 1923. Other visitors have been Admiral Byrd, Mayor LaGuardia, Queen Juliana, Presidents Truman and Eisenhower, Konrad Adenauer and Nikita Khrushchev.

29

CHARTERED BANK OF LONDON

The most opulent banking room in a city with many opulent banking rooms is the old Trading Hall of the former Merchants Exchange at 465 California Street, now occupied by the Chartered Bank of London.

The building was designed by Willis Polk while working in the San Francisco office of the Chicago firm of Daniel Burnham. Fifteen stories high, it was the tallest building in the financial district when it was built in 1905. The structure survived the earthquake and fire because of its sturdy steel-framed construction.

The exterior is faced with brick from the fourth floor to the top; the first three stories of the facade are of Tennessee granite. At night the facade is illuminated by solid-bronze lamps, surmounted with bronze eagles' heads, which were designed by Julia Morgan.

A splendid barrel-vault lobby with skylight leads to the banking room. The granite pilastered walls retain their original lighting fixtures. Each wall is lined with models of great sailing ships from around the world.

Over the years, the interior of the Trading Hall, also designed by Miss Morgan, deteriorated badly.

The 38-foot-high coffered ceiling had been hidden by a false ceiling. Murals depicting the high seas and boats in and around San Francisco Bay by William Coulter, a former artist with the old *San Francisco Call*, were also in a poor state.

Today the Trading Room has regained the glory of its early years as a result of a half-million-dollar, year-long restoration project undertaken by the bank. Gold leaf was applied to the original main ceiling and the coffered ceilings in the vaulted alcoves at the sides of the room by three experts in the dying art. The old maritime murals have been restored to their original colors. Italian craftsmen labored for three months to vein and polish the imitation-marble pillars that support the entablature around the skylight. (The bases of the pillars, however, are of real marble from the historic gold-rush town of Columbia, California.)

The entire restoration was done under the direction of buildings manager Otto Haake, who knew Miss Morgan and had access to her detailed building plans. The bank has been given a special award by the California Council of the American Institute of Architects for its fine efforts.

Opposite, left: The main entrance. **Opposite, right:** The old Trading Hall. **Above:** The lobby.

SHELL BUILDING

The Shell Building, at the corner of Bush and Battery Streets, is one of the city's handsomest skyscrapers, and was one of the tallest in the financial district until it was engulfed by the taller structures built in the 1960s.

It was erected as the Western headquarters of the Shell organization. The architect, George W. Kelham, also designed the Russ Building and the Main Library in the Civic Center. Of Kelham's two skyscrapers, the Shell Building is more successful than the Russ Building, for it breaks away from the more common "Gothicized" towers of urban architecture of the 1920s.

Sixty-six concrete caissons extending to a depth of 80 feet provide foundation support to resist any wind and earthquake stress. The structural frame, erected in 58 working days, set a Pacific Coast record for speed of construction of Class A buildings. It was completed on April 16, 1930 at a cost of $4 million.

The 29-story tower is flanked by ten-story wings to the north and west. "Setbacks" at the twentieth and twenty-second stories provide a pleasantly tapered profile. The exterior facing material is rough-textured terra-cotta colored a light sepia. The spandrels, (the areas between windows in the vertical direction) are of cast concrete tinted blue-green.

The modified Art Deco architecture of the building is highlighted by lobby ornamentation. A geometric bronze grille covers the entrance doors. The elevator doors are of cast bronze with low-relief decorations extending to the ceiling, from which a lantern hangs. Spaciousness is achieved by a detailed dome.

The upper lobbies of the building have travertine marble wainscotting on a black and gold marble base. Corridors were originally panelled with Philippine mahogany, now removed.

The building is no longer Shell's Western headquarters; the move to Houston was made several years ago. It now belongs to the Brothers International Corporation.

Below, left: An elevator door. **Below, right:** The entrance. **Opposite:** The Shell Building.

18

STOCK EXCHANGE

The design of the Pacific Coast Stock Exchange, Pine and Sansome Streets, is a successful combination of Classical and modified Art Deco. The architects were J. R. Miller and Timothy Pflueger; sculpture was by Ralph Stackpole. The steel-and-concrete structure, faced with gray California granite, was opened on January 4, 1930.

The ten Tuscan pillars at the Pine Street entrance provide the Classical note. The colonnade is surmounted by a granite parapet with two Art Deco octagonal medallions containing carved relief figures which depict man's mastery of land and of sea. Another medallion, representing the building industry, appears on the Sansome Street facade.

The Pine Street entrance is flanked by twin 21-foot-high, 75-ton pylons, with "moderne" sculptures facing the street. Stackpole started work on the twin granite sculptures in 1930 and finished two years later. They represent "Man and His Inventions" and the fruitfulness of "Mother Earth."

The Sansome Street wing of the building contains the administrative offices. The twelve-story structure has a granite relief sculpture over the entrance which depicts the "Progress of Man," in which a central male figure rests his hands on the world. On each side of him are smaller male figures starting on life's adventures, one on land, the other on sea. In the background are representations of lightning, rain and a rainbow—eternal forces to be encountered on man's journey.

Left: One of Ralph Stackpole's two pylons at the Pine Street entrance. **Above:** "Progress of Man," by Ralph Stackpole. **Opposite:** The Pine Street entrance to the Stock Exchange.

19

ROYAL GLOBE
INSURANCE COMPANY BUILDING

The Royal Globe Insurance Company, Pine and Sansome Streets, has the distinction of being the first fireproof building in the financial district. Built just before the 1906 blaze, it survived without internal damage.

New York City architects Howell and Stokes designed the Georgian-style structure's facade using the contrasting materials of brick, white marble and terra-cotta. The marble first and second stories are highlighted by an entrance surmounted by figures of a lion and unicorn supporting a bronze-and-marble clock. Originally the group was flanked by smaller clocks giving the time in other parts of the world. There is also a street clock in front of the entrance.

The third story is of marble and brick; the next five are of brick laid in English bond, which alternates courses of headers (the short end of the brick) with those made of stretchers (the wide length of the brick). The top three stories of the facade are of terra-cotta. White windowsills and other white trim provide a unifying note to the whole building.

The interior vestibule has been restored to its prequake elegance. Five marble architraves (doorways) came from the dismantled Torlonia Palace in Rome, built by Carlo Fontana for the Bolognetti family in 1680. The palace was dismantled to make way for the Victor Emmanuel Monument.

Opposite: The main entrance after the 1978 cleaning and restoration. **Above:** The Royal Globe Insurance Company Building.

20

BANK OF CALIFORNIA

The Bank of California's 21-story tower at California and Sansome Streets, built in 1968, is the third structure of great dignity to be built by the bank at this location.

The bank was founded in 1864 by Darius Ogden Mills and William C. Ralston. The first building, erected in 1867, was a rather Baroque two-story edifice with tall arched windows framed with marble columns, a stone balustrade and bronze balconies and railings. It quickly became the greatest financial institution in the West before the Panic of 1873. The bank survived the panic, but the building itself was demolished before the quake. Walter Bliss and William Faville were the architects for the new building, a granite structure seen here in front of the tower. Completed in 1908, it was modeled after the Knickerbocker Trust Company of New York City, a McKim, Mead and White collaboration. The New York structure still stands, but has been altered beyond recognition.

The ornate Corinthian-columned building has a facade of Tennessee marble. The main banking hall has a coffered ceiling 54 feet high. The 35-foot-high windows are separated by Corinthian pilasters. At one end of the hall is a clock topped by marble lions designed by the sculptor Arthur Putnam. In September, 1968, on the eve of its sixtieth birthday, the building was declared a city landmark by the city's planning commission.

In 1963, while the headquarters bank was slowly outgrowing this building, it was decided to expand by retaining the older structure, and erecting a new building next to it. The new tower, designed by architects Anshen and Allen, is walled with gray fluted-concrete panels intended to harmonize with the older building. To maintain a sense of proportion, it was limited in height to four times that of the earlier structure. For greater unity, the high rise was cantilevered 30 feet over the other building, tying the two together. Anodized aluminum sashes and bronze cornices repeat the stone of the older 35-foot bronze window grilles.

Left: The 1908 building of the Bank of California stands in front of the tower built for the bank in 1968. **Opposite:** The 1908 building.

21

BANK OF TOKYO
(California First Bank)

Directly across the street from the Bank of California, on the corner of California and Sansome Streets, stands the Bank of Tokyo (California First Bank). Completed in 1977, the building was designed by Edward Bassett of the architectural team of Skidmore, Owings and Merrill.

The 20-story, 330-foot-tall bank was designed to be in complete harmony with the Bank of California. Both banks relate to each other in their columned, vertical thrusts. On the exterior of the First Bank are 12 columns, nine feet in diameter, three to a corner, that rise to the top, where they gracefully recede into the roofline. The columns are of steel, surrounded by precast concrete. The wide windows on each story are surrounded by concrete panels of white and gray. The banking room is spacious. Rising 40 feet, it is 125 feet wide and is decorated in glass and chrome. Large windows provide views of the older bank, 75 feet away. The sculptured effect of the building is furthered by hundreds of small, conical ornamental projections at the base of columns.

The Bank of Tokyo stands on the site of the Alaska Commercial Building (1908); walrus heads, anchors and ropes from the former now adorn a low wall near the entrance to the new bank.

Below: Two decorations from the old Alaska Commercial Building. **Opposite:** The Bank of Tokyo (California First Bank). (*Photography by Lindsay Huffman*).

22

RUSS BUILDING

For thirty years, the largest and tallest office building in the city was the Russ building, 235 Montgomery Street. Completed in 1927, it was architect George Kelham's second skyscraper, the first being his Standard Oil Building, a block away.

Rising 31 stories, the Russ Building is constructed of a steel frame with brick and terra-cotta facing. Kelham followed the style of contemporary architects in other major American cities by designing his building in the Gothic manner, which is not only evident in the arched doorway and ground-floor windows, but also in the vaulted, tile-floored lobby. At the upper levels, a series of graceful setbacks relieves the monotony of unobstructed verticality.

The history of the site is interesting. On March 1, 1847, the transport *L'oo Choo* sailed through the Golden Gate. On board was Emanuel Charles Christian Russ and his family. Shortly after their arrival, Russ purchased the Montgomery Street property for $37.50 at a city auction. He then bought timbers from the old ship and with the planks built a house on the newly acquired land for his family of twelve. The three-story, block-long Italianiate-style Russ House hostelry was completed on the site of the old house in 1865. Burned to the ground in the fire of 1906, it was replaced with a three-story office building, which was razed to make way for the present E-shaped structure.

Below: The elevator lobby. **Opposite:** The Russ Building. (*Photograph by Gabriel Moulin, courtesy the Russ Building*).

23
MILLS BUILDING

The Mills Building, 220 Montgomery Street, escaped the earthquake of 1906 because of its durability—the older part, constructed in 1891–92, was one of the first steel-frame and masonry structures in the city. It is important today as the best, and perhaps only, San Francisco survivor of the Chicago School of architecture, which permanently changed the skylines of American cities around the turn of the century. It is also one of the very few Richardson-Romanesque edifices in the city. Daniel Burnham, designer of the original structure, was undoubtedly influenced by Sullivan and Adler's architecture in Chicago. But the Mills Building is a powerful statement in its own right.

Darius Odgen Mills, for whom the building was named, came from New York State to strike it rich in California in 1849, where he first became a successful merchant, then a banker. In 1864, he became president of the Bank of California. He later helped finance the construction of the Southern Pacific Railroad, and was involved in mining and real-estate investments. In 1890, he decided to build the present structure. Before he died at his 42-room mansion on the Peninsula in 1910, Mills had become a philanthropist, having built three hotels in San Francisco ". . . where the poor man with 15 cents in his pocket might find a clean, well kept room and bath, and decent surroundings for a little time at least."

The Mills Building is a four-part structure: the main (original) building; annexes A and B (1908 and 1918, respectively); and Lewis Hobart's tower (1930). All of the additions harmonize with the original.

The main building of the Mills Building complex is ten stories high. The first two have a horizontal emphasis and are constructed of white Inyo marble from the Inyo Marble Works of Keeler, California.

The appearance of strength and additional height is achieved by the strongly marked lines of clustered pilasters in the piers, which rise from the fourth to eighth floors. A series of arches tops the ninth-floor windows. Between the ninth and tenth floors is a frieze running across the entire facade. Squat Ionic pilasters flank the tenth-floor windows. From the tenth floor upward, the exterior is brick and terra-cotta.

The arch on the Montgomery Street side bears the hallmark of the Richardson-Romanesque style. It is carved in acanthus-leaf and egg-and-dart molding and rests on polished marble columns.

The interior is lavish. The lobby flooring is of Roman travertine marble; the base of the wainscoting is of Belgian black marble. From the wainscoting to the ceiling are murals of San Francisco.

Left: A detail of the main entrance. **Below:** The Mills Building.

DOWNTOWN/UNION SQUARE
(Shopping District)

Like the Financial District, ninety percent of the shopping district was leveled in the earthquake. Of its principal structures, only the Flood Building and Citizens Savings and Loan Building escaped major damage. Today, vigilance by the city's preservationist groups has guarded against changing the architecture of Union Square, the vibrant hub of the shopping area. Despite the destruction of the Fitzhugh Building early in 1979, the Saks Fifth Avenue Store, to be constructed on that site, will blend with the rest of the buildings on the square.

24

450 SUTTER

Of 450 Sutter, Irving F. Morrow has written, "This building approaches more closely than any executed one I know the European (theoretical) conception of what an American skyscraper should be."[1] For, while the skyscraper is America's unique contribution to the world of architecture, the Art Deco movement, which had its origin in the Paris Exposition of 1925 (Exposition Internationale des Arts Décoratifs et Industriels Modernes), exerted enormous influence on the design of these structures, in which it reached its most arresting manifestations. Also referred to as the Style Moderne, Art Deco is an eclectic style emphasizing geometric designs—stepped triangles, zigzags, geometrically stylized human and animal figures, clouds, waterfalls and especially Indian, Aztec and Mayan motifs.

450 Sutter, San Francisco's one truly great Art Deco skyscraper, was designed by J. R. Miller and Timothy Pflueger, using Mayan motifs, particularly on the lower floors. (They have no symbolism, being used for purely decorative purposes.) The building was finished in 1930, at the beginning of the Depression. It was to be the city's last skyscraper for two decades.

The base of the building, around the entrance, is faced with embellished bronze and cast iron. An iron marquee, surmounted by a three-story cast-iron "Mayan" grille, protects the bronze doors.

The rather small lobby has Mayan designs in the aluminum spandrel over the entrance and incised patterns in the aluminum elevator doors. In turn, the elevator doors blend harmoniously with the polished red Levanto marble surfaces above. "Streamlined" chandeliers hang from an unusual stepped ceiling done in silver leaf and picked out in colors.

Unique rounded ("wraparound") corner windows are used from the seventh story up. Although steel-frame construction had eliminated the necessity of using solid chunks of masonry as load-bearing walls, few architects up to that time had deviated from using traditional squared corners. Aside from their aesthetic quality, however, the windows not only emulated a San Francisco architectural tradition—the bay window—but also provided much-needed light for physicians' and dentists' offices. Unadorned piers give the building a strong vertical thrust.

The unusual V-shaped windows along the sides, the accompanying spandrels of the same shape, and the adjacent rounded piers create a wave-line appearance, particularly when viewed from below. The facade is a classic example of the curtain wall.

[1]Morrow, Irving F. "A Modern Classic, 450 Sutter St., San Francisco," *California Arts & Architecture*, June 1930, p. 46.

Opposite, left: The corner wraparound windows. **Opposite, right:** Detail of the facade. **Above, top:** The main entrance. **Above, bottom:** Cast-aluminum elevator door. **Right, top:** Stepped ceiling and incised spandrel pattern in the lobby. **Right, bottom:** 450 Sutter.

25

HALLIDIE BUILDING

During his long career, Willis Polk provided San Francisco and its environs with many distinguished structures, both domestic and commercial. Undoubtedly his most noteworthy is the Hallidie Building at 130 Sutter Street. Named after Andrew Hallidie, the inventor of the city's cable-car system, the structure was completed in 1918.

The revolutionary quality of the Hallidie Building is its all-glass curtain wall, the first of its kind in the country applied to a multi-storied urban structure. Although there were earlier buildings that used glass as a facade, the concrete supports were always set out; the Hallidie's supports are set in, allowing an unobstructed glass facade. These reinforced concrete pillars have attached cantilevered guides, which in turn support the glass. Each of the seven floors, except the ground floor, is three windows high. The stories are indiscernible from the outside.

An almost incongruous note to the facade is the cast-iron ornaments, friezes and the fire escapes—nineteenth-century ornamentation on a twentieth-century glass plane. They serve an aesthetic purpose, however, in relieving the facade of blandness and giving it a sense of design and movement. The ironwork is painted blue and gold, in deference to the school colors of the University of California, the original owner of the building.

Opposite: A detail of the cast-iron fire escape. **Above:** The Hallidie Building.

CITIZENS SAVINGS AND LOAN

Perhaps the most sophisticated of San Francisco's downtown prequake structures was the Mutual Bank at Third and Market Streets. Now occupied by Citizens Savings and Loan, the sandstone bank was designed by architect William Curlett and completed in 1902. Built in the French Renaissance style, the 12-story building has tall, arched windows on the ground level; handsome dormers with scrolled decorations projecting from a copper-trimmed mansard roof; a high, pedimented framed entrance; and crestings at the roofline.

In 1964, an adjoining structure, the Flannery Building, was razed to make way for a new annex which contains the complex's elevators and lobby, as well as office space. The annex, designed by Clark and Beuttler, is compatible with the main building. Although its exterior is faced with red brick, it harmonizes well because of its similar height and its copper roof, which recalls the roof configuration of the main building.

WELLS FARGO BANK, UNION TRUST BRANCH

Architect Clinton Day's Union Trust Company, now the Union Trust Office of the Wells Fargo Bank, is easily the most elegant small building facing Market Street or Grant Avenue.

Completed in 1910, the building followed on the heels of Day's equally elegant City of Paris Department Store, built in 1909. Both structures reflect his Ecole des Beaux-Arts classical training. The bank has three bays fronting Market Street and five on Grant Avenue. Rectangular windows on each of the street entrances are flanked with consoles (brackets) supporting dentilled cornices, which in turn support balconies for the second-floor windows. Both the Grant Avenue and Market Street entrances are flanked by bay-garland columns. A strong cornice with modillions marks the roofline; beneath it is a frieze. The whole structure is surmounted by a balustrade. The interior is equally impressive. Corbels, columns, friezes and volutes in the Classical manner add strength to the cream-colored walls.

More space was needed after the 1924 merger of Wells Fargo Bank with the Union Trust Company. Two new floors were added by suspending the floors on iron girders from a tall crane and attaching them to the roof, a practice considered revolutionary at the time. The *San Francisco Chronicle* was enthusiastic in describing the operation, and concluded with this somewhat immodest statement: ". . . they [the floors] look as though they might outlast the mighty Coliseum, a matter of a couple of years old."[1]

The present well-kept appearance of the Bank is due to a half-million dollar restoration program undertaken in the mid-1960s, which included repainting the sash and ironwork, and cleaning the exterior granite walls.

[1]"Bank Hangs New Floor In Air By Heels," *San Francisco Chronicle*, February 13, 1924, p. 4.

HELGA HOWIE BOUTIQUE

The only structure designed by Frank Lloyd Wright for San Francisco is the Helga Howie Boutique, originally the V. C. Morris gift shop. Located on Maiden Lane, the short but handsome alley just off Union Square, the Howie Boutique is an example of what an architectural genius can do with a cube.

When the store opened in 1948, it aroused considerable interest among architects and laymen, for here was a shop that had no large glass window to advertise its wares. Instead, the exterior facade is a wall of buff-colored brick. The only opening to the street is an arched, cave-like entrance.

The left side of the archway is of brick laid in "stack bond," brick laid with all vertical joints continuously aligned, instead of the usual method, in which they are staggered. Each successive stack projects slightly forward into the entryway to create a tunnel-like effect, reducing both the height and width of the entry. On the right side of the entry is a planter box, above which are bands of curved glass which rise to meet with the brick at the crown of the arch.

The interior space is even more striking. From the ceiling, Plexiglas discs and half-bubbles filter the natural light so that it won't fade materials. It also eliminates the harsh glare of the sun shining through the skylight above.

Around the shop a gradual ramp, seemingly rising to meet the light from above, leads to the mezzanine. The lone hanging plant, suspended from the ceiling, provides a grace note to the entire scheme.

The boutique is one of Wright's most important buildings. Elizabeth Mock has stated: "The shop is in a way an autobiographical sketch of the architect, from the arch-pierced masonry wall in the grand tradition of Richardson and Sullivan, to the spiral ramp of the museum for New York."[1]

(The spiral ramp, incidentally, was not a precursor of Wright's famous Guggenheim Museum, built in 1959 in New York City; both the Morris shop and the museum were on his drawing board as far back as the mid-1940s.)

[1]Mock, Elizabeth. "China and Gift Shop by Frank Lloyd Wright," *Architectural Forum*, February 1950, p. 82.

Left: The interior. **Below:** The entrance. **Opposite:** The exterior of the Helga Howie Boutique.

29
BANK OF AMERICA

The Bank of America's Number One Powell Street bank was originally the headquarters building of A. P. Giannini's Bank of Italy. When it opened in 1921, there was considerable criticism that it was an imitation of the city's University Club. Irving Morrow, an architectural critic of the day, quickly dismissed such criticism in these words: "... there is one fact that is commonly overlooked ... if the University Club is admittedly a club building, the Bank of Italy is unquestionably a banking institution. This, after all, is the most important aspect of the matter...."[1]

The architects were Bliss and Faville. The style of the bank might best be described as Italian Renaissance-Baroque. The handsome white granite facade is enriched with a dentilled cornice, volutes and a balustrade. The Corinthian-columned main entrance is surmounted with a bas-relief by Giovanni Portonova which depicts a central female figure, personifying the bank, enthroned between Ceres, representing agriculture, on one side, and Mercury, representing commerce, on the other.

The Bank of Italy was founded by Giannini and his stepfather. According to the W.P.A. American Guide Series on San Francisco, Giannini was able to turn the disaster of 1906

to his advantage when he managed to remove the assets and records from the bank before the advancing fire reached them. They were hauled to his San Mateo home in wagons from his step-father's commission warehouse and camouflaged with a heap of fruits and vegetables. The Bank of Italy was the first in the city to be re-opened.

In 1909, Giannini launched a drive to create a state-wide system of branch banks on the theory that branch banking was the best safeguard against failure of banks in a single crop or single industry regions because they served to spread the risk.[2]

His theories proved valid. By 1940, the Bank of Italy, now renamed The Bank of America, was already the nation's fourth-largest bank. It soon became the world's largest.

[1]Morrow, Irving. "The New Bank of Italy, San Francisco," *Architect and Engineer*, vol. LXVI, October 1921, p. 49.
[2]*San Francisco; the Bay and Its Cities.* Compiled by Workers of the Writers Program of the Northern California Chapter of the Works Progress Administration. New York: Hastings House, 1940.

30
HIBERNIA BANK

When the Hibernia Bank Building, 1 Jones Street, was completed in 1892, Willis Polk described it as the most beautiful building in the city. It was designed in the Beaux-Arts tradition by Albert Pissis, the classically trained architect who also designed the President's Home at the University of California at Berkeley.

The bank was founded in 1859 as the Hibernia Savings and Loan Association, and was originally located on Market and Post Streets. For many years it was the only financial institution on Market Street.

Designed solely for banking purposes, the present two-story building has a gilt copper dome surmounting a circular portico entrance, with four Corinthian columns. The floor of the portico is inlaid with a mosaic representing a mariner's compass card.

A colonnade of Corinthian pilasters lines the McAllister Street facade, interspersed between tall, rectangular windows. Pediments flank both ends of the building and the sides adjacent to the entrance. A classic balustrade crowns each side of the building. Tall, arched windows, with keystones and separated by pilasters, face Jones Street.

The interior has a ". . . vaulted dome of glass in the center. The ceilings are beautifully ornamented and tinted yellow and gold. Wainscoting is of siena marble beautifully panelled and polished, and the warm tint is in fine harmony with the surroundings."[1]

Like many of the once gleaming-white Market Street buildings, Hibernia's granite facade has weathered to a dull gray, but the old bank building still exhibits dignity and strength, despite the decline of its neighborhood.

[1]*Real Estate Journal*, December 1892, p. 2.

31

FLOOD BUILDING

The stately Flood Building, Market and Powell Streets, was the largest office building in the West when it was completed in 1905. The architect, Albert Pissis, designed the rounded-corner building in a style reflecting his Ecole des Beaux-Arts background. Both the Powell and Market Street facades have Corinthian, Doric and Ionic pilasters, balconies, scroll brackets and dentilled cornices.

The twelve-story structure was built by heirs of the Comstock silver-mine millionaire James C. Flood, and named after him. It stands on the site of the Baldwin Hotel and Theatre, named after Flood's contemporary E. J. "Lucky" Baldwin. The latter building, completed in 1877, was destroyed by fire in 1898.

The fire of 1906 took its toll on the Flood Building, blackening the granite walls and breaking the windows; for many years traces of discoloration could be seen near the entrances.

32
ALCAZAR THEATRE

The Alcazar Theatre, 650 Geary Street, was designed in 1917 by T. Patterson Ross as the local Shriner's Islam Temple. The horizontal banding of the first-floor wall, the horseshoe arches on the tops of the windows, the elaborate patterned decorations above the second-floor windows and the dome are motifs common to the mosque. Minarets would make it complete.

SOUTH OF MARKET/MISSION

Market Street is the wide thoroughfare that is acknowledged as San Francisco's main street. "South of Market" became the city's first industrial area. It also boasts two federal buildings that are among the finest in the nation. The adjacent Mission area was selected by the founding fathers for its sunny and hospitable location. Now inhabited mainly by blue-collar and Hispanic residents, the Mission was originally laid out in the 1870s and 1880s.

33

MAIN POST OFFICE/U.S. COURT OF APPEALS

The most opulent interior of any public building west of the Mississipi belongs to the Main Post Office/U.S. Court of Appeals Building on Mission and Seventh Streets. The Italian Renaissance structure was designed by James Knox Taylor, supervising architect of the Treasury Department, and completed in 1905. The cost of the white granite-clad building was $25 million. The extravagance of the interiors was made possible by a drop in the price of steel after funds had been appropriated by Congress in the 1890s for construction of the building. None of the money was returned to the Treasury, and the surplus was spent lavishly.

Upon entering, the visitor is confronted with walls of black-and-white veined marble (pavonazzo) with a base of verde antique (green, mottled marble),

capped with the green Maryland marble of the groined and vaulted mosaic ceiling. The floors are of intricately designed ceramic tiles.

The third floor is even more elegant. The main corridor is a long colonnade of 48 white Italian marble pillars. The plaster-decorated, arched-and-groined ceiling contrasts with the shining marble walls. The circuit courtroom walls are of pavonazzo; the base is red Numidian marble from Africa. Ornamented bronze doors have architraves of marble carved in fruit designs. The back of the bench has a colored marble-and-glass design inlaid on marble. The floor is of ceramic tile; the ceiling is illuminated by three art glass ceiling lights.

The judge's chamber adjoining the courtroom has East Indian mahogany bookcases. The marble is red Numidian. The walls are panelled with West Coast mahogany. Another judge's library is finished in California curly redwood, with rich carvings. The heavy, beamed ceiling has intricately detailed consoles. The circuit courtroom of appeals has an elaborately coffered ceiling, side-wall pillars of marble, and decorated plasterwork.

The building withstood the earthquake and fire, although the sidewalk and street sank several feet, as it was built over a streambed. As a result, the present structure stands higher than the original sidewalk level.

Opposite: The Main Post Office/U.S. District Court of Appeals. **Above:** The circuit courtroom. **Right:** The third-floor corridor.

34

JESSIE STREET SUBSTATION

The now-vacant Substation of the Pacific Gas and Electric Company at 220 Jessie Street was built in 1887 for a predecessor of the San Francisco Gas and Electric Company. In 1905, ownership of the building passed to the Pacific Gas and Electric Company. The following year additions and alterations were designed by Willis Polk, working in the office of Daniel Burnham. Polk's sensitive handling of brick and terra-cotta for an industrial building of this type marks a change in direction from his usual brown-shingled residences. (According to the Landmarks Preservation Advisory Board, the work on the structure was the first effort by PG&E to make its substations civic ornaments.)

The building has an outer wall of unreinforced brick, 16 inches thick, and an inner structure of steel columns. The main entrance is a tall, arched doorway, the top portion of which is a window with cast-iron mullions; underneath are metal doors.

To the west is a similar entrance topped by a terra-cotta statuary group of cherubs holding garlands of fruit beneath a torch. Below is the date, 1907—the year this section of the building was completed. Seven evenly spaced windows are located east of the entrance, framed in terra-cotta and nicely counter-pointing the Baroque door. Like the main entrance, the windows have cast-iron mullions. The building is currently listed in the National Register of Historic Places.

Below: Terra-cotta group over the west doorway. **Opposite:** The Jessie Street Substation.

OLD MINT

The oldest stone building in San Francisco, one relatively untouched by the ravages of the fire of 1906, is the Old Mint on Fifth and Mission Streets. Completed in 1874, the U.S. Branch Mint was designed by Alfred B. Mullet in 1869. Mullet was then the supervising architect of the Treasury Building in Washington, D.C. and had also designed the post office in Portland, Maine, and the customhouse in Portland, Oregon.

Gold coming into San Francisco had necessitated larger quarters than the 1854 mint on Commercial Street could provide. Property for the new site was purchased for $100,000 in 1867. A thorough search throughout the West for a block of sandstone large enough to be carved into the six 30-foot columns called for in Mullet's plans proved futile, and resulted in a trip to Canada, where a flawless 440-foot-long, 22-foot-deep block was found in Newcastle Island, British Columbia. The stone contained lime, among other components, and is particularly durable.

Early in 1870, the first of three schooners arrived with the initial load of 8000 tons required for construction. When it was completed in 1874, the *San Francisco Call* predicted that "the fire department will have little trouble quenching any conflagration that may arise within its walls, and unless an earthquake gives it subterranean quietus, it bids fair to stand up for centuries." (The *Call* was somewhat prophetic; in 1906, after the quake reduced the building's surroundings to rubble, the ensuing fire, which caused far more damage, lapped away at the exterior, and the building was saved through heroic efforts of the citizenry and soldiers nearby, who kept watch over the bank's $200 million.)

The San Francisco branch quickly became the principal mint in the country, surpassing those in New Orleans and Philadelphia. As late as 1934, fully one-third of the nation's gold reserves was held at the Mint. In 1937 operations were moved to a larger building that had been constructed on Market Street. In 1976 a $2-million restoration project, undertaken in 1972 by Mary Brooks, director of the U.S. Mint, was completed. Today, the Old Mint is a museum operated by the National Park Service.

The pedimented Doric-columned building was one of the last Greek Revival public buildings to be constructed in the United States. The sandstone upper floors are mounted on basement walls of Rocklin granite. The interior walls reveal the original red brick in the basement; the upstairs rooms are plastered. The interior has high-ceilinged rooms with tall gold-painted pilasters with egg-and-dart and palmette moldings, a common decorative device of mid-nineteenth-century architecture. Cast-iron railings flank the stairways; one of the main rooms has an elaborate cast-iron balcony. Windows are protected by iron shutters—the same ones that held off the flames of 1906.

36
BAHA'I TEMPLE

The Baha'i Temple, 170 Valencia Street, was originally the home of the Independent Order of Foresters. Completed in 1932, it is the best small Art Deco building in San Francisco.

PACIFIC TELEPHONE & TELEGRAPH BUILDING

The city's first really modern skyscraper was the Pacific Telephone & Telegraph Company Building, 140 New Montgomery Street. Architects of the 26-story structure were Miller, Pflueger and A. A. Cantin. At the time of its completion in 1925, it was the largest building on the Pacific Coast built for the exclusive use of one concern.

As seen from the front, the PT&T Building appears rectangular; from the west, an open letter "L"; from the north, it appears to be a solid block. Terra-cotta speckled to resemble gray granite was used for the facade.

Pflueger designed the PT&T building along the lines of Eliel Saarinen's second-place prize-winning drawings for the Chicago Tribune Building. As such, it represents a break with past buildings, having no horizontal cornices to impede its ascent to the top. "The $3,000,000 structure is designed free from the fussy application of motifs of classical antiquity in sheer solidity with jagged face and tapering silhouette, resembling the stormy pinnacles of the Sierras."[1]

An impressed architectural critic of the day gives us his feeling of awe in these words: "These softly shaded and sharply shadowed alternating vertical piers, especially when seen sideways and blended into one fluted shaft of sheer masonry, create an extraordinary illusion of both light and lightness to behold."[2] And, in a bit of overstated rhetoric: "They seem no longer clay blocks piled up from the solid ground, but dimmed sunbeams shot from fretted clouds."[3]

An unusual feature of the piers is the rounded pilasters at the bottom which give way to Egyptian lotus-leaf splayed capitals near the top of the tower. Two stone eagles on each side of the top of the central tower looked down over the city. (These have been removed for earthquake safety.)

[1]Miller, J. R. "S.F. Tallest Skyscraper to be 26 Stories," *San Francisco Chronicle*, March 26, 1925, p. 6.
[2]Cahill, B. J. S. "Telephone Building, San Francisco," *Architect and Engineer*, December 1925, pp. 50–52.
[3]*Ibid.*

Opposite, left: The entrance. **Opposite, right:** The building as seen from the southwest. **Above, top:** Detail of the tower showing two empty panels formerly occupied by carved eagles. **Above, bottom:** Detail showing lotus-leaf finials. **Right:** The Pacific Telephone & Telegraph Building.

38

MISSION DOLORES

Mission San Francisco de Asís, known as Mission Dolores, 320 Dolores Street, is the oldest building in San Francisco. The site on which it was built was alongside a stream which an exploring party under the leadership of Fr. Francisco Palou named Arroyo de los Dolores (Stream of Sorrows). The name has been attached to it ever since. Begun in 1781, the mission was dedicated on April 3, 1791. It was the sixth of twenty-one Franciscan missions established by the Church up and down the California coast from San Diego to Sonoma in the eighteenth and early nineteenth centuries.

The architecture is an eclectic blend of Classical and Spanish. The main entrance is flanked by two pairs of unfluted Doric pillars. The pillars support a wooden balcony above which are six pilasters of differing heights. Between the middle four pilasters are the three original bells, one dated 1793, the other two dated 1797; they now ring only during Holy Week.

Part of a large quadrangle which has long since disappeared, the church was constructed by Indian laborers of sun-dried adobe, four feet thick. Unlike many of the other missions in California, Mission Dolores' walls held up well during the three earthquakes it has endured. The building has no nails; manzanita pegs and thongs of rawhide hold it together. Indian craftsmen painted the redwood roof beams of the sanctuary, using pigments made from vegetables and clays of the San Francisco peninsula, in chevrons of white, red and gray. The roof tiles were also made by the Indians.

The mission was secularized by the Mexican government in 1834 and the grounds became the location for bull and bear fights and other entertainments. Such activities stopped when the Mission was returned to the Roman Catholic Church in 1857.

In 1920, Willis Polk, who had restored many prominent buildings after the 1906 quake, renovated the mission to its original state by removing some previous alterations. Its simplicity is in stark contrast to the parish church standing next to it, built in the Churrigueresque style—a Baroque Spanish style of the seventeenth and eighteenth centuries.

Left: Mission Dolores (Mission San Francisco de Asís). **Above:** A detail of the interior.

CIVIC CENTER

Van Ness Avenue, the main artery bisecting the Civic Center, was originally one of the most elegant thoroughfares in the city, lined with Victorian mansions of all descriptions, which have now disappeared. Franklin Street, which parallels Van Ness, was similarly developed, and still boasts a few of the grander houses. In this century, the northern end of Van Ness Avenue became the city's auto row, and the southern end, above Market Street, its stately Civic Center.

CIVIC CENTER

The plan for San Francisco's great civic center, considered by many architectural critics the best and certainly the grandest in the nation, was originally conceived by Daniel Burnham. Burnham's previous plan had been the great "White City" of the World's Columbian Exposition of 1893 in Chicago.

His plan for San Francisco, from Lake Merced to Telegraph Hill, was full of fountains, parks, terraces and handsome buildings. The grandiose civic center, when completed, would have rivaled Baron Haussmann's Paris of the 1860s. The plan was presented to the city fathers one day before the Great Earthquake. Unfortunately, its costs would have been a strain on the pockets of San Franciscans and it was shelved during the post-quake civic frauds of Boss Abe Ruef and Mayor Eugene Schmitz.

39

CITY HALL

In 1911, under a team of architects led by John Galen Howard, the city supervisors selected the present site for the new city hall a few blocks west of the poorly constructed old city hall, which had been badly damaged in the quake.

A bond issue of $8.8 million was passed for construction of the new buildings. A prize competition for the design of the new city hall, in which only San Francisco architects were allowed to compete, was set up in 1912. The winner was the team of Arthur Brown and John Bakewell.

Brown, born in Oakland in 1874, attended the University of California in the 1890s. He was a student of Bernard Maybeck, who encouraged Brown to attend the Ecole des Beaux-Arts in Paris, then the world's leading architectural school, as Maybeck had done before him. Shortly after his schooling, Brown set up practice with John Bakewell, Jr. In 1908, the team designed Berkeley's City Hall in an updated Classical-Baroque style.

The cornerstone for San Francisco City Hall was laid on October 25, 1913 and the building was completed in December 1915. It is constructed of steel, with a facade of California granite. The style is French Renaissance Revival.

The large rectangular building, 400 by 300 feet, is set off by a Roman Doric colonnade. Over the Van Ness Avenue entrance is a pediment with figures representing Wisdom, the Arts, Learning, Truth, Industry and Labor. The Polk Street facade, nearly identical, has a pediment with figures representing the riches and resources of California navigation and commerce.

A great green ribbed dome, rising 307 feet above the ground, is crowned with a lantern. Surrounding the drum of the dome is a Doric colonnade separating tall mullioned and pedimented windows.

Blue-and-gold doors set off the entrances, which are flanked by a pair of elaborate blue-and-gold lanterns. The wrought-iron central balcony is decorated with acanthus leaves, fasces and gold lion's heads and is supported by atlantes.

Beneath the dome is a vast rotunda, rising four floors, with various entrances and corridors. The great hall is highlighted by a fan-shaped flight of stairs flowing down from the main gallery. On each of the four sides are huge piers, which rise to meet four pendentives (concave spandrels leading from the angles formed by two walls to the base of a dome) which in turn form a ring. From the ring emerge columns which support the dome.

The building is rich in detail—masks and garlands appear over the doorways; barrel vaults have statuary underneath. Medallions adorn the ceiling, and shields, wreaths and crests appear in profusion. Tall bronze standing lamps complement the bronze-and-iron designs of the railings. Doors and other woodwork are of Siberian oak. The rotunda sculptures were done by Henri Crenier; the interior design by Louis Bourgeois. Both Frenchmen were schooled at the Ecole des Beaux-Arts; both died in World War I.

Above: The rotunda. **Below:** City Hall.

CITY HALL (*continued*)

Below, top: Detail of lamp standard and fence. **Below, bottom:** The old City Hall as it appeared in the 1890s. (*Courtesy The Bancroft Library*). **Right, top:** Detail of the facade. **Right, bottom:** Main entrance with atlantes.

MAIN PUBLIC LIBRARY

Completed in 1916, the Main Public Library was the third structure to be erected in the Civic Center. (The City Hall and Civic Auditorium preceded it.) Andrew Carnegie donated nearly one quarter of the building's cost of $1,152,000. The architect chosen for the job, George W. Kelham, Jr., was later to design some of the city's early skyscrapers—the Russ Building, Shell Building and the Standard Oil Building.

Like the City Hall, the library is constructed of California granite reinforced with steel. It is also designed in the Renaissance style. On the second story of the facade is an Ionic-colonnaded loggia with statues by Leo Lentelli fronting large arched, grilled windows. The statues represent Art, Philosophy, Literature, Science and Law.

The interior uses some travertine marble, but locally produced imitation travertine is also used, especially in the vestibule and surrounding the long main stairway which leads to the second floor. It is of special interest, for overhead is a handsome coffered ceiling and on each side are murals representing scenes of California, executed in 1932 by the Italian artist Gottardo Piazzoni. Other artwork in the building includes murals by Frank DuMond, originally executed for the Panama-Pacific Exposition of 1915.

WAR MEMORIAL OPERA HOUSE

Built in 1932, the War Memorial Opera House was, with its twin, the Veterans Memorial Building, among the last structures to be completed in the Civic Center. The opera house was designed by Arthur Brown, Jr., in the same architectural style as the other buildings in the Center. The facade is constructed of terra-cotta; the steps, columns and base, of granite.

Perhaps the most outstanding architectural feature is the foyer. Rising 38 feet from the marble floor is a magnificent gilt, coffered ceiling. Stairways ascend at each end of the foyer to upper levels. Doric-columned balconies at each end of the lobby mezzanine allow spectators to view the audience below during intermission. Handsome classic doorways lead to the auditorium, but there is no grand stairway.

The auditorium has none of the traditional semicircular tiers. On the side walls are three well-recessed window openings, filled with square and octagonal stone tracery. The simplicity of the building is a gesture to Wagner's opera house in Bayreuth, which reflects the composer's objections to the use of an opera house as "a place to see and be seen." In addition, some of the San Francisco Opera's trustees objected to boxes because of their aristocratic connotation. (As a concession to traditionalists, however, there is a single row of boxes along the side wall.)

Relief figures of two Amazons riding horses by sculptor Edgar Walter adorn the spandrels of the proscenium arch. The ceiling is punctuated by a huge chandelier, 27 feet in diameter. The design of the flowing, geometrical piece gives the appearance of a huge illuminated star.

Above: The War Memorial Opera House. **Opposite:** The foyer.

42

OLD MASONIC TEMPLE

Bliss and Faville's Masonic Temple Building at the corner of Van Ness and Oak Street seems to have been inspired by the thirteenth-century Palazzo Vecchio in Florence, complete with imitation medieval machicolations at the roofline—a parapet projecting on brackets with openings through which boiling oil could be dropped on an enemy. The cream-colored six-story structure, completed in 1913, was originally faced with Utah marble; it is now covered with stucco. Several Masonic symbols decorate the exterior, the most prominent being the corner statue of King Solomon.

The lobby floors are made of Tavernelle and Tennessee marble. The original carpets in all the rooms were designed by the architects. The large commandery room on the third floor, surmounted by a dome rising 85 feet from the ground, is decorated with religious murals by the great California master of the arts-and-crafts movement, Arthur F. Mathews. A new Masonic Auditorium was built on Nob Hill in 1958. Though much larger, it is less interesting architecturally.

Opposite: The old Masonic Temple. **Above:** Corner statue of King Solomon. **Right, top:** The entrance. **Right, bottom:** Upper window.

43

BOARD OF EDUCATION

The building at 135 Van Ness Avenue, now occupied by the Board of Education, was completed in 1927 as the High School of Commerce. Architect John Reid, Jr. (who was the San Francisco city architect in the 1920s and also designed Mission High School, Everett Junior High and Sherman Elementary School) was inspired by the University of Salamanca in Spain and incorporated Renaissance and Gothic touches. The building is sheathed in terra-cotta and decorated with interspaced diamond-shaped tiles of green and pink. Flanking the main entrance are corbels with humorous grotesque figures representing medieval men of learning.

Left: Detail of corbel. **Below:** Board of Education.

44

SAINT PAULUS CHURCH

Saint Paulus Lutheran Church, 888 Turk Street, was built in 1894. Designed by J. A. Kraft, it is a scaled-down wooden version of Chartres Cathedral. The interpretation is a free one, however; it lacks the thirteenth-century stone and stained glass and the position of the two steeples is also reversed. During the immediate aftermath of the 1906 fire, Saint Paulus was used as the First National Guard Emergency Center, serving the needs of 13,000 victims.

45

BRITISH MOTORS

The automobile showroom at 901 Van Ness Avenue, completed in 1926, was one of two Packard agencies in the Bay Area designed by Bernard Maybeck for an Earle C. Anthony dealership. (The other, a 1928 structure fronting on Lake Merritt in Oakland, was destroyed in 1974 to make way for a high rise.) The building is now owned by British Motor Car Distributors, Ltd.

Like the motion-picture palaces of the 1920s, auto showrooms of the period could be sumptuous and dramatic. With that in mind, Maybeck designed the structure in the Classical style to reflect the aristocratic quality of the Packard. On the exterior, seven pink unfluted Corinthian columns support a large frieze. Sculptured architraves complete with consoles (scrolled supports) topped by a flat cornice cover the two doorways on Van Ness Avenue.

The two-story showroom within has columns of red Numidian marble with white capitals and sculptured entablatures which support the coffered ceiling of Florida cypress.

The elegant showroom aroused considerable controversy when it opened. Most people felt it was a handsome addition to San Francisco, but it was reported that one New York businessman said that "he would hesitate to put up a building so pretentiously unique as this one for fear his customers' minds would be concentrated on the architecture and decorations, rather than upon the merchandise."[1]

In an opening-day radio speech, Maybeck asserted: "Only in San Francisco does this building happen, and only at this hour—it may be good art; it may be bad."[2]

[1]Battue, Zoe A. "The Man on the Street Speaks of the Packard Building," *Pacific Coast Architect*, August 1927, p. 35.
[2]*Ibid.*

Opposite: British Motors. **Above:** The showroom.

46

ST. MARY'S CATHEDRAL

The new St. Mary's Cathedral occupies Cathedral Hill, bounded by Geary, Gough, Laguna and Eddy Streets. Completed October 15, 1970 and dedicated the next year, it replaces the old, ungainly red-brick Gothic Revival cathedral on Van Ness Avenue and O'Farrell Street, which burned to the ground in 1962.

The $7.5-million cathedral is a collaborative effort of local architects Angus McSweeney, Paul A. Ryan and John Lee. Helping them plan the structure was Pietro Belluschi; the engineering consultant was Pier Luigi Nervi. The project consultant was William Schuppel of San Francisco. In the spirit of the reforms of Vatican II, the cathedral was designed so that the congregation would be closer to the clergy, who would face them in one large unobstructed space.

Belluschi's design is basically that of a hyperbolic paraboloid, the exterior of which is a towering cupola supported by four huge pylons. The interior's ceiling is supported by four V-shaped vaults terminating at floor level at each of the four corners.

The lofty interior is pierced by thin, rectangular stained-glass windows done by the artist and art historian Gyorgy Kepes. Measuring only 6 feet wide, they extend 130 feet, forming a gigantic cross. The four colors of the glass—dark blue, light blue, yellow and red—symbolize water, air, earth and fire, respectively.

Perhaps the most intriguing element in the striking building, from the spectator's viewpoint, is the baldachin, or altar canopy. Sculptor Richard Lippold designed this shimmering piece from thousands of aluminum rods rising 100 feet in 14 tiers. Small air currents keep the rods continuously moving. Seen from different sides of the cathedral, they reflect the colors of the stained glass. The entire work is suspended from thin wire threads attached to the cupola.

The cathedral is clad in gleaming white travertine marble, which contrasts strongly with the colored paving of the great plaza which surrounds it. The bas-relief grille sculptures over the front portal were executed by Enrico Manfrini of Milan.

Opposite, left: Portal bas-relief sculpture. **Opposite, right:** The baldachin. **Above:** St. Mary's Cathedral. **Right:** Stained-glass windows by Gyorgy Kepes.